Ease of Life

RAYMOND GRANT

authorHOUSE®

AuthorHouse™
1663 Liberty Drive
Bloomington, IN 47403
www.authorhouse.com
Phone: 1 (800) 839-8640

Published by AuthorHouse 06/23/2016

ISBN: 978-1-5246-1246-7 (sc)
ISBN: 978-1-5246-1245-0 (e)

Library of Congress Control Number: 2016909364

Print information available on the last page.

Any people depicted in stock imagery provided by Thinkstock are models, and such images are being used for illustrative purposes only. Certain stock imagery © Thinkstock.

This book is printed on acid-free paper.

Table of Contents

The Father of Light

❖ Oh Great 2
❖ A Light to Plume 3
❖ Blizzard Stuff 3
❖ Beginning That Thing 4
❖ Clandestine Night 4
❖ Close the Corner 5
❖ The Norm of Life 6
❖ Curses Bleed 7
❖ Day-less Light 8
❖ The Greatest Spectacle 9
❖ Discomfort 10
❖ Closed Error 10
❖ Fabulous Foresight 11
❖ Sustained by Grace 12
❖ Grace is Possible 13
❖ Holy Night 14
❖ Silent Night 14
❖ Hut, You See 15
❖ Home Settlers 16
❖ Great Deception 17
❖ Matter Me Up 18
❖ Night at a Glance 18

❖ King's Ring 19
❖ Strong Love 20

Stagnant or Flowing

❖ Abandoned Fields 22
❖ Apple Picking 23
❖ Battlefront 24
❖ Community House 25
❖ Positive Negatives 25
❖ Engineer Life 26
❖ Golden Arch 26
❖ Guilt by Suspicion 27
❖ Harassing Colors 27
❖ Hidden Glory 28
❖ Cheap Grapes 28
❖ If You See, I See 29
❖ Little to Nothing, Over-the-Top 29
❖ Melted Away 30
❖ Motor Oil Crossing 30
❖ Prince of Life 31
❖ Little Timber 31
❖ Sometimes We Die Little 32
❖ Spoken Letters 33
❖ Un-Strived 34
❖ What are We Afraid of? 35
❖ Unspoken Emergency 36
❖ You too can Eat this Bread 36
❖ Pointed Mercy, Directed Grace 37
❖ Bloodshed Eye 37

❖ Sinner of a Life 38
❖ Streets of Dreams 39
❖ This Only.. 40
❖ Deeper Side of Love 41

Peace Offering

❖ Clear the Mind - Ice the Cold 44
❖ Not Too Distant Future 45
❖ Butternut Scotch 45
❖ Break In...46
❖ Choice.. 46
❖ Trappings of Sin...47
❖ Community House 47
❖ At the Corner of His House and Deliverance ... 48
❖ A Dance at the Beach..49
❖ Coffee Stop 50
❖ Pie Eating Contest 50
❖ Harbinger Boys 51
❖ Death Rope Romance...51
❖ Dream Happy 52
❖ Happy Medium 52
❖ Dreamscape...53
❖ Dueling Swords 54
❖ Dynamite Loud 55
❖ Excuses, Excuses 56
❖ Fantasy Land 56
❖ Flavor-able Candy 57
❖ Gimmick Play..57
❖ Greed 58

❖ Protein 58
❖ Highway Climb 58
❖ Little Pillows...59
❖ Little Ricky.. 60
❖ Drumline 60
❖ Dangling in Distress 61
❖ Misting 61
❖ Moments Less Remembered......................62
❖ Species Allowed (Continues) 63
❖ Splattered Paint..................................... 64
❖ Steel 65
❖ Tip My Hat to the Tea Maker 66
❖ Vapors 67
❖ People Pressure Me................................. 68
❖ Many Mouse.. 68
❖ Tailgate Party..69

Passionate Life

❖ Shall We Weep or Shall We Cry 72
❖ Strong vs Weak.......................................73
❖ Upset Alley 74
❖ Frenetic Love 75
❖ Secretary Love 76
❖ Watered-down Controversy......................76
❖ Pickled Fences 77
❖ How Prideful are You............................... 77
❖ Pressure Counts......................................78
❖ Still Open 78
❖ Pumpkin Patch 78

❖ Wood Stock 79
❖ Another Day in Paradise 79
❖ Count Down.......................................79
❖ Passionate Life 80
❖ Prosperous Pigeon 81
❖ Prosperous, Mighty.............................81
❖ Paddle Me 82
❖ Sugar Cane 82
❖ Seed Little 83
❖ Penguin Laughter................................ 84
❖ Possession of the Soul.......................... 84

Surviving on Make-Believe Or Awakened to Truth

❖ Surviving on Impulse............................86
❖ A Place to Tell....................................86
❖ A Step...87
❖ Small Bananas.................................... 88

❖ Closed View of Society 88
❖ Craters...89
❖ Decision Makes 89
❖ Gratifying Flesh... 90
❖ Deliverance Table... 90
❖ Discomfort Corner 91
❖ Hollywood Shuffle..92
❖ Peaceable Laugh..92
❖ Indecent Exposure 93
❖ Masters of Living 94
❖ Miserable City 95
❖ Potential Fun..95
❖ Sacrifice Low 96
❖ Satisfy Spoil...97
❖ Sometimes We Test Patience 98
❖ Beast Master..99
❖ No Propaganda Press Release.........................99
❖ Son-less Life 99
❖ The Nature of the Endgame 100
❖ Orleans Way...101
❖ Needles..102
❖ Doorway 102
❖ The Ease of Life..103

A light for the rejection of night

His light is the theme

Without, darkness exists

Live to be enfolded, enriched by

The light of God's grace

All other means of existence–

Are but vain attempts leading to dissolution

The Father
of Light

Oh Great

Great is the Lord
His majesty
His splendor
Who knows him?
Who accepts him?
He exists
The God above
The God of love
There is no other
Words cannot and do not begin to express-
The wonder of his frame
The glory of his name
The depth of his might
He is Lord of all
There is no other
Unless
Unless we fail to confess
But even in this
There will come a day that all will recognize
There is no other
Let his name be spoken
For He is Lord of all
The Great God above

A Light to Plume

A light to plume all windows of hope
Brighten the day
Brighten the day
Let the glory shine for light is given...
In you
That by you
Others will see

Blizzard Stuff

The stuff of life hoped for but not seen
The dream
The dream of things hoped for but not received
Receive
The things of life
The ways of life
What is life except what you make of it
Settle the storm and receive them...
By faith

Beginning That Thing

Begin that thing
Start a cause
If the cause has already begun-
Give a hand to see it through
Whatever the cause
That thing
Begins and ends with you
Each will have a part to play
Whether we begin a cause for change
Or contribute to a work already begun

Cause something to happen
We are here to make a difference
Cause the light to shine
For it's in you to do so
If you believe

Clandestine Night

Night without light so bright as failure exists
What is it that we often miss in the midst of this?
Failure to be moved by Him
To be led by Him
To leave all for Him
Shine the light and subdue the night
For in the day you have been made to prosper

Close the Corner

Some will listen and refrain
Some will listen yet invite saucy entertainment
At what cost?
At what cost will you refrain the ear-
And entertain the heart with thoughts of deception
Purposely, of course not
But little by little a gravitating flow takes place
The less one learns-
The more one is enticed by the sways of darkness
We would rather be told
As opposed to being
What we're supposed to be
In being who we are supposed to be in Christ
We become an enemy to the adversary
Staunchly defended against the lure of defection

The Norm of Life

Life without life, no life
All who live live, but not all for me
All who breathe dare
But will I receive insult or glory?
The norm of life is not the life I have plan for thee
Life and greater life exists because of me
Find me and find life everlasting

Dare to cause a cause without a cause and what is there?
Nothing
Things begin and end but by what cause?
What purpose and reason?
Can it be in one's believing?
Believe in me
And by me
For me
The greater gain will be had
And the glory thereof
For God alone

Curses Bleed

Curses bleed the life out
What's in can be seen without
Without many seeing
Red they bleed to a deed succumbing to death
It's the curses that pull on the lifeline
Tainting it with worldly satisfaction and indulgence
With an underlying play
Devious in a way
Devilish if you will
In an attempt to _____
Bleed red, bleed red
Yet, don't die in vain
For the curses rehearse the curse
Without knowledge of the truth
The truth brings light and purifies the blood
Nullifying its effects to spread and destroy

Day-less Light

Light with no day, no way
How can some say they've found a way?
Have they not known the Christ?
He is the only way
So how is it that they see light?
No, it's night for day
And a false light is what they see
Many have not known the light
Because they have not known Him
The Christ
The King
From whom many hide
Shy away from
And their daylight-
Is as dim as the seam
Which draws closed with curtains

The Greatest Spectacle

The greatest spectacle is the devastation of man
No one sees
No one knows
There are many who pretend not to know
But all will be without excuses
Men losing their lives
With an opportunity for life at hand
Who is the man?
The man who will leave his ways for His way
Hear what I say
Opportunity calls ...
For a different way
A way to life everlasting
In hope that one might avoid
The great spectacle to be

Discomfort

Discomfort
Lack of rest
Who rests except the weary?
Not my rest
For there is a test of faith
And for the enduring
True rest and no discomfort
Discomfort your discomfort by choosing faith
Faith above circumstances
Faith above the seen
Far above the reports
Faith above the fables for the the truth will stand
Will you stand...
By faith

Closed Error

Error of any kind is an error
Maybe the fine not so fine
In time
It will be defined by the scales of justice

Fabulous Foresight

To see the unseen through a dream
Or maybe a vision
What holds the heart and will not tear apart
The love within
Family? Friend?
No, Him!
The one who holds the world-
In the palm of his hand
Come and see that you might see
Instead of allowing darkness to cause blindness
A vision
A dream it seems
No, reality in the spiritual-
Is more real than the reality presumed
Seek the father of light
So the days of darkness can be turned to light
And thy way clear

Sustained by Grace

My favor, your hope
The way to is through the Son
Grace makes faith available when answering the call
And there is no greater call-
Than to accept life through Christ
With it purpose and being
And doing more than what one is seeing
There is a world to know and a life to lose
There is also the world to lose and a life to gain
Should one choose to live for Him
The Christ

Grace is Possible

Not only is grace possible
It's real
It exists because I exist
And the only reason many still do exist
Have we missed the point?
In me, there is favor
In me, there is life everlasting
I provide hope for another day
A better way

~ ~ ~ ~ ~ ~ ~ ~ ~ ~

A changed life for Him
That one might live to live again, in Him
All is well that ends well
Not so

~ ~ ~ ~ ~ ~ ~ ~ ~ ~

Grace is sufficient for the sufficient ones
The ones who choose to live well in Him
The Christ

Holy Night

A holy night for all is the call
Yet many times it goes in vain
A rest for the weary who labor
Those who favor me will labor righteously
Oh, what a night, the holy night
A night for day when day will be taken away-
To begin anew
This is the call therefore call
That many will come
For the Son will rise again
Has risen
Never to be night again
As it is
With Him
For He reigns

Silent Night

Silent night, holy night
Yet the night is but one day
And what about "That Day"
We give overwhelming praise to the night
When it was the day
That truly changed our existence

Hut, You See

You see me
Nah, you see me
You've seen what I can do
You see me
I've given all for you
You see me
What do I have that I have not given?
You see me
Once, twice, three times
You see me
Before the beginning and in the beginning
You see me
Have you not known me?
You see the stars
You see me
You see the moon, the constellations
You see me
What you have not heard you have seen
Therefore you see me
Whether you acknowledge me is up to you
But if you've lived to see a sunrise, you've seen me
Yet the sun will set
Do you see me?
I call out for you to know me-
So when the sun finally sets-
You would have already known me
All of me was put into creation
And all you desire is made possible -
By coming to know me

Home Settlers

A home to be is a home found in me
Settle for a moment to think, if only for a moment
About all that's been given, applied
There is no grace where there is no God
Now if God
Will you not settle in what you believe
Without...Imperfection rattles the brain
Insane
Insane way to live
Unsettled, as if roaming without destruction
Looks like a lifetime wasted
Unless settled
In him

Great Deception

The great deception is the false truth-
About who God is
And where deliverance comes from
The great deception says
It's alright to be alright
Without cause, without way
And so many lead astray...
The heart not devoted to love
Oh, the Great God above
Lies are sown in every fabric of society
And without the truth-
People are constantly being deceived
Even some of my people
For failure to allow the holy spirit to lead
The great deception is not without its failings
Wake up to see me in the truth of my word
The truth is before us
If we would wake up to seize the day in truth
Instead of standing back waiting-
To receive lies disguised as truth

Matter Me Up

Matters of the day
No concerns
For they are kept through Him
Long live the king
For His mercy endures to keep
Keep Him at heart
And the matters of unrest
Lay at rest
At His feet

Night at a Glance

Light the night sky with light from above
His light so bright
But the night without
Without Him
Is but a shadow at best, fading unknown

King's Ring

Crown with glory and might
Power to fight
And overcome
By the one who reigns
Still
Much more than this
Is to exist
In His presence eternally
Free from failure and insufficiency
For all is sufficient in Him
The one above all
Who rejects none
Unless He is the one-
Rejected

Strong Love

Strong love
His is strong, lasting, everlasting
Never failing
What has He revealed?
If received, then live in that
His word never fails
In obedience, fear will show reverential love
Experience love
And have a greater appreciation for love
His love
Never merely ours to give
But giving more of ourselves
That our lives will be the sacrifice of self-
For His will to take center stage
When we understand this
We will truly understand what love is
Sacrificing for another
For the greater good

Stagnant

or

Flowing

Abandoned Fields

Fields left behind but firmly rooted
Some never leave
You have left
Never return through doubting and limited thinking
Now is time for making way
For better, brighter days
Plan to succeed and you will
Thought pattern for life must change
And it has
And you will
The doors to the left often call thee
The doors to the right often tempt thee
It's the door to the front that most concerns me
Will you continue to follow me and see?
For I am not swayed in my promises
Don't make unexpected detours
Or you can be driven off the path never to return
A path is set to follow
Find my word and follow
Matters of the heart come and go
But truth never leaves, lies or deceives
Follow my word
And abandon fields of deception set to destroy

Apple Picking

Picking apples
Up, down
Some up, some down
Some up to no good
Some up for righteousness
Tasty even
This is the aroma of the faithful
Living high above the plain of decay and ruin
For there is life in the vine
As long as one remains connected to the vine
Hang on for dear life for it's a challenge
A battle even
* * (see John 15:4) * *

Battlefront

Lines are drawn
Evil has set its mark-
With groundwork in spiritual origin
To be marked by him-
Is to be sin-driven unconsciously
Second nature being the first
It's the spirit of the man
Not the man
Yet the man which we fight
For the battle is not him but the spirit
And it's the spirit we should fight
With kingdom words
God's written word
Our defense in the circumference of faith

Community House

Community is where it's at
Not at home, in house
Some live there
Some play there
Some pray there
All is well that they stay there
But the community calls
Therefore go

Positive Negatives

See the seen
Beyond the scene
What have you seen?
Do you still see?
Yet, beyond the scene
Things present are but for a moment
That which lies ahead will always be ahead
Yet yours
When you learn to grasp it with your seeing

Engineer Life

Life to be had
Life to live
One life past this life
And the life left to give
You have all
Therefore give all
For in giving you have received all
Life

Golden Arch

Can you define hope?
Voice my opinion
Can you see justice?
Stand friendly
Can you bring joy?
Only by my grace
Can you incline my heart?
If it's by your will Lord in release of mine

Guilt by Suspicion

Guilty according to the rules of the land but free
Guilty of being a Christian, still believe
The landscape is changing
I am not moved
Don't you be moved
For the world will try to change your way
Seductively or overtly but it comes
And when it comes
Do not deny me or hide your faith
Do not agree with the dictates-
That cross the boundaries of faith
For in doing so one becomes an accomplice

Harassing Colors

Colors of glory
Colors of shame
Some to live for
From some, refrain
All colors are not golden
As in pleasing
Though tempting
Pursue the pure
So the seduction of the shameful can be withstood

Hidden Glory

Is there such a thing as glory unseen
Surely an inappropriate remark at best
Sometimes God's glory is seen-
In the lives of his people
Yet hidden in that
Some never walk in His will as they are called

Cheap Grapes

Food for thought
In thought
Maybe not
Grapes spoil apart from the vine...
Becoming rotten to the core

Grapes of unbelief and only profitable for the moment
But for a lifetime if the lifeline remains in the vine

If You See, I See

If you see I see
But what is there to see?
Not so much a play on words but of a hard truth
I see what you believe for
Now, what is it that you see?

Little to Nothing, Over-the-Top

If the little we have were enough-
Would we continue to cry out for more
If the excess we've gained was lost-
Would we lose hope
Things gained are obtained for a time
But should not possess one's time
Let the little press us to excel in abundance-
Without allowing abundance to create a nature-
Which repels the presence and activity of God

Melted Away

This way, that
For Him, praise
In spite of that
When time is spent toward Him
In honor of Him
The trials of life become less significant
And in reality taken care of-
Because the honor of God is graced-
Above the praise of problems

Motor Oil Crossing

Some cross the wet and defect
Not purposely
But there's oil on the road
Some cross the line
Not winning, yet finished
But do not receive the prize
Best not to be diverted if possible
And as much as possible
Keep your eyes on the prize and win

Prince of Life

A life to live
One of great wealth, prosperity
Privilege and expectation
A prince for a time though a king in the making
A time indeed

Little Timber

Help! Help!
To keep from hurting while falling
A call, great...
But how desperate is the cry?
Some won't cry-
Until overwhelmed by the cares of life
Almost past feeling
Be prepared to hear, then do
Make a difference
For the cry is great though seldom heard

Sometimes We Die Little

Sometimes we die little
Less than we were made to be
And much more often than we think
How much is too little or not enough?
We barely settle for enough
And sadly, often-times little is our portion
Few things seen, revealed
Few things mentioned and forced closed by waiting
And waiting without a favorable expectation
Nothing happens if nothing happened
What will you make happen?
Or will you settle for little as if that's your lot?
Some never take their head out of the pot
Wishing upon a star but never getting anywhere
Failing to realize the star is in you who believe
No wishing, no wanting
Declaring
As if it's in you to have what you want
But looking for help to receive
And receiving through believing
What holds you back from moving forward?
Remember, the little man thinks little
If you are a star, then rise above the plains of life-
That you may become more than a man-
Without a cause
Without a destiny or hope
Rather one with the prevailing winds of change
One changes in order to become more,
Receive more
Refuse to wait with abandon desires
In the process of time

Refusing to live
We die to small deeds

Spoken Letters

Letters of words
Who hears?
Who is supposed to hear?
What words! What words!
The words of life to keep from strife
Yet it comes
The words of wisdom to keep from failure
Yet it comes
The words of progression
Many don't learn the lesson-
Until its too late
Yet we must speak
Speak the word whether it is received or not
Whether change is seen or not
Speak the word
And allow me to do the rest

Speak words that matter
Words pertaining to change, increase, and deliverance

Un-Strived

A connection lost in sitting
Are we forgetting...
The lost
At what cost do we wait?
Will it be too late?
Count the time if it can be counted
Once lost then lost for good
Yet we are at peace while others unrest
A valuable commodity-
Is to savor the time as the greatest opportunity...
For change
Not in thought but in doing
Being
For it affects change in others
Unless we're unmoved by their fate

What are We Afraid of?

A taste of grace to save a life
A soul made over in sin
Who can win
Them over
If not you then who
Do we demise our franchise-
For a bitter-sweet taste of victory incomplete
Complete my will and the effects are lasting
The gift, the prize, everlasting
Don't taint the glory by haphazard faith-
And for failure to boldly carry out my word
The strings are long yet attached
Are you not attached
Then sound the alarm of faith-
For those who cry aloud while saying nothing
As desperation crouches at the door

Unspoken Emergency

An emergency arises with light glaring
But there are no lights to be seen
An emergency arises with one screaming
Yet there is no voice to be heard
An emergency
A dangerous game when it comes to saving a life
Shall we not call
Shall we not call
For the outcome will be upon us

You too can Eat this Bread

Why do we exclude others from the fold-
If we are trying to win
Why do we establish separation-
Which further deters our friends
Who was His life lived for if not the sick and the lost
And those who need us most
Yet, through rejection
We separate the lost

Pointed Mercy, Directed Grace

My mercy to all
Grace abounds
That I may gain some though many are called
I have called for the faithful-
To reach a people by whom I am unknown
Make me known
That I may be glorified

Bloodshed Eye

An eye for blood are some
Some have not known the way of the Lord-
So they remain thirsty
Thirsty for something that will not satisfy
Blood begets blood, begets more blood
Where will it stop? And when will it end?
The bloodthirsty perishes
While the faithful live on
Remaining eternally

Sinner of a Life

Why not the life instead of the sinner-
When sinning involves a lifestyle
Maybe the focus should be on the nature-
Instead of the person
Let's not forget the motion
The notion
It begins somewhere
If we can help overcome the nature-
We can change the person
Shine a spotlight on the issue
Instead of the individual
On the sin as opposed to the sinner
Look deeper, closer
Do you sin?
Then that is what we strive to change
Refrain from
Open the doors with love
Love in spite of
Give light by the Lord of Light and His word-
And He will bring a change through us
But by Him

Streets of Dreams

Streets of dreams
Living, but not there
Dare roam to be known and seen as different
Different from the norm, from the scene
And from what's seen on the streets
In doing so a spark is lit
In becoming a torch for one's life
Though not seen clearly
A path is brought to life
Others cling to the street
With it's hustle and bustle
Which speedily and deceptively draws out life-
Until it's too late for change

Dream and give light
For prospects and prosperity are driven by
Imagination, desire, and passion for change

Sweet dreams or street dreams
One becoming reality & lasting if willing to leave
Some never leave
When drawn to the guise of life

This Only

Only do this and you win
Don't give in to sin
For it seeks to sift
But I have given you a gift
The Holy Spirit residing
If He abides will you abide?
Abide in me as I am in you
The key to victory over sin
Don't drink the water until the trough is dry
Sin remains if you entertain it
Some fall victim to its embrace-
Only to discover a day of reckoning
Abide that you may abide and remain free

Deeper Side of Love

The deeper side of love-
Is knowing I love in spite of
There are no changes-
That change my feelings toward you
In the same way
You should not allow your feelings
To change toward others
Love as I love you
This is the deep side of love
To love in spite of
For this I have kept you
To reveal me to others by the way you live
Show the character of Christ
To love the unloveable
To love the unreasonable
To love the hateful, vengeful,
backbiters and accusers
In this you give God glory

Elevate our love song
With a vibrant display of affection
And with all sincerity, forgiveness

Peace Offering

Clear the Mind - Ice the Cold

Cold weather comes in
Ice, wind, the snow
So cold, so cold
The ways of life can be harsh sometimes
At what point do we fight back?
And is it in us to do so?
I have placed fight in you
To succeed and not fail
To prosper beyond measure-
In spite of life's challenges
Clear the mind by knowing I am with you
I am with you and I do not disappoint
Life has no degree from which I cannot deliver
In spite of how cold it seems

Not Too Distant Future

The not too distant future begins today
Today put all your troubles away
Your future
Future worries
Past failures
What light there is to see
Can you see?
From night to light means rescue

It's at hand when you believe

Butternut Scotch

A taste of summer
A lonely retreat
A day gone by
But not one of defeat
A day of old, a day of old
Let by-gone be by-gone
And live in sobriety of today

Break In

Break in
No slip in
That's offensive
We refuse to allow the enemy to steal-
What is rightfully ours
But how will we know what is ours-
If we are not His

Choice

Choice of deliverance
To be set free eternally
Or to be captured as a lost soul with no hope
Hope in me
There is no other way
Choice of delay leading to regret-
Or choice based on what you were told-
"The choice" which reveals true happiness

Trappings of Sin

The not so sweet, sweet
And what remains, will be
The lasting for the temporal
For the temporal only lasts for so long
Then comes to naught

Community House

Community is where it's at
Not at home, in house
Some live there
Some play there
Some pray there
All is well that they stay there
But the community calls
Therefore go

At the Corner of His House and Deliverance

Some remain at the corner but never come in
Some know the way
See His signs
Yet what keeps them?
It's a release point
Oftentimes a breakpoint
But at what point...
Will you allow His to become yours
That you may become His
Maybe that's it
Many will not entertain the thought of losing self
Denying self
While they fail to
Deliverance remains at a distance
Near, yet far, though close

A Dance at the Beach

The beach of life
The throes of life
What is left of life?
And how many ways are there to enjoy life?
No strife if lived for him–
Though stormy weather will arise
A day at the beach is no picnic
Yet it can be very enjoyable
Entertained at the beach
By waves, by sand
But what remains to stand?
Surely not the land
For it comes and goes and comes again
With men the same
Yet they fail to see the dividing flow
No dancing
Just another day of waves capturing one's attention

Coffee Stop

Stop for coffee
Stop for a drink
Stop to think and get one's life in order
One way to relax yet many more exist
What about the plan?
Is there something we missed?
Is it all for his will or ours
That we spend time in thought
The plan of tomorrow starts today
But the perfect plan
Is to allow His plan
To have its way

Pie Eating Contest

A contest of will
Ours for His
Will we continue to fill our face
With the grime of life
Or settle for a better life?
A life without pie in the face
A life without embarrassment, shame or regret
No sticky residue left from this walk, this life

Harbinger Boys

Boys will be boys
Yet I call men forward for the times
It's not too late, never too late
Where there is devastation and terror-
I have sent some to set many free
To work a work during time
In time of need
The boys will come
But it's the men we need
To perform great deeds on behalf of the hopeful

Death Rope Romance

A cliff is but a cliff
A myth is but a myth
This turn for that turn
And what a turn we often miss
His life for this life
Without
A rope of destruction
A noose if you will-
In a dance with a gravitating pull

Dream Happy

Happy dreams
Happy times
Will dreams alone be your comfort?
Or will you search in discovery of more?
Be more
And in being, live...
In reality of dreams dreamed

Happy Medium

Happy is being content
A motion to notion temporary pleasure-
With no lasting effects
Listen to the little and receive little
Listen to the lasting and live in abundance
Little is found in happiness
For it has no lasting grace
Joy is what to strive for
For in it the heart is kept safe

Dreamscape

Escape from reality for a while
Sometimes the child
As in no cares
Yet reality sets in to confront
Dream still
Things before you need not hold you hostage
Dream to get away
Dream in hope
Dream but importantly plan
In doing so-
One sets matters in motion for change

Dueling Swords

One against the other won't win
There is no winning in fighting-
Unless it's the fight of faith
All other victories are but temporary
A victory won in faith is eternal, supernatural
Victory is a black eye in the sport of fighting
Only in that, it greatly ages one once finished
The fight of faith on the other hand builds one up
More confidence with each victory
More knowledge and strength enduring
Here a win, there a win but who really wins-
In the end?
Only the ones who come to know Christ
"The King"
"The Savior" of men

Dynamite Loud

Loud for the course of way
Hear what they say
The faithful as they come
From no one to one
No longer none
But one in righteousness dispelling truth
For truth is found in them
By Him
The Christ
In their voices are the ways of life, so listen
"The word" brings freedom
From earthly attachments-
And everything binding
Hear their words
For it's a cry for freedom
A cry out of love

Excuses, Excuses

I have many of them
And likely to know most of them
For I have perfected the art of nothing
Doing nothing
And saying anything possible to continue in nothing
Excuses, excuses
Always one
One without while crumbling within
Who wins?
Surely not the man of lies

Fantasy Land

Dreaming in a boat of no hope
Yet seeking the unbelievable
Why believe if no hope?
Or is there hope in believing?
The richest dreams come true by faith
And yes, some work too
To dream and wonder without any action-
Is fool's gold
Dreams become reality
When hands are put to the plow
No action, no hope, no dream to come true
In the end, only a fantasy

Flavor-able Candy

Candy, a taste to excite the palate
More lost at what cost
And the cost in view is the taste
No disgrace
Enjoy the flavor of life until it loses its flavor
Know that some flavor spoil the vine-
And leave us empty
Drained even, though tasty
Sometimes the bad is not so good-
But the tasteless has no life at all

Enjoy life, but not to the detriment of your soul

Gimmick Play

A place for the home is the house
Yet we look not at the home
Instead the house of cards
Gimmick plays if you will
Trying what you will-
Instead of applying what we know-
Can leave a most undesirable taste
Stick to the truth for it works
All other fashions are but plays left to chance

Greed

Greed
An oil-based lipstick kinda love
Temporary gloss for a time which looks nice
But in the end
No dice

Protein

Protein for life
That's right
What was is and shall be
Life

Highway Climb

Climb success and it will take you far
Stay with the Jones-
And you will leave with the Jones
Stay with me and success will never leave

Little Pillows

Little fellows, little fellows
Lay to rest your best
For it comes in thoughtfulness
Your mind upon me
Your needs, no grief
Yet worry clouds your day
Though I bring the sunshine-
It is often cast away-
By thoughts of life rather than thoughts of me
Little pillows, little pillows
Little rays of light for the clouds of day
In this way little is seen
Little hope
Cast down the thoughts-
And take up a new pattern of living-
So your arms can be wide open to receive

Little Ricky

Our neighbor, our friend
One who was and is not
One who is and is to be
One with me
You will see
No state of mind can stop my will-
If the man or woman is willing
It goes for all
All who heed the call
Of grace

Drumline

Hear the heart
Slow, fast
Fast as it goes
So are my thoughts
Ever before you
Always of you
Until there is no more of "you"
Instead, all of me
Then the heart will be as one

Dangling in Distress

No mess
Instead the test
The test of life
Whether you will choose life
Or death
All come to trials
It's the ones who realize-
Where their help comes from-
That break through the disturbances of the day
Hear what I say
Hang on
For there is hope
Hope to believe that you might believe in me
And the dangling will be no more

Misting

Misting, as in a light flow
Forgo the plans of tomorrow for today
In that way
Decisions are better weighed
Against the scales of life-
And the fruit thereof will be multiplied exponentially

Moments Less Remembered

A moment less remembered
Is the moment once spent in plastic
Protected yet frail
Moments which drain out life
Few things to do in this
Personal plans are not honored in this
The plan of another is the goal
A life lived for another
And the personal is restrain, suffocating

There is a bond to break
Hopefulness in this
Beyond the plastic embrace is a space for redemption
To air, to air is to breathe life and receive life-
So one's life will obtain its passion

Species Allowed (Continues)

Species
A different breed
Can a breed be set apart
Set in order to produce that one might reign
Who sets the order and who follows
To follow is to lead
Therefore follow that one might lead...
As in leading one to the fullness of grace
Who sets the pace-
For this is the race of life
Who wins? Who loses?
And what is the price?
To forsake Him is to forsake all
And to be forsaken in the end
Born and set apart from destruction
In order to reign
But often forfeited for this life's glory
Still the option exists
To reign and rule
Or be subdued by the dictates of life

Splattered Paint

An array of colors not by design
But designs can be seen in them
How so?
Spectacular art on display
Wherefore is the brightness of day understanding?
To know the meaning
To see a frame
To establish a perception of what it seems
Vivid colors, those of bright
Some not so
As in dim and darkness of night
One's design is of the mind
Made to see
Unless the seen is taken figuratively
There is meaning
Search for it
There is a message to be understood
If seeking to understand
Oftentimes-
The message does not roll out on a platter
Many times it's as the splattering of paint
Sometimes unseen until intently searched for
Then known

Steel

Genuine relief
Peace
Piece of steel to boot
Less steel more real
Not the solidness of a structure
But rather the whole is what I'm after
Not one so steeped in tradition
But rather one who would give an ear to listen-
To what the spirit has to say, today
Too often we live off of yesterday's morsel-
When that banquet has ceased
New lessons, new instructions
More wisdom for a needed time
And the time is now, today
Unmoved is to be unchanged
And no change is not good
Sometimes we stood to stand but stand no more
Survival
(Surviving instead of thriving)
Approach the curve with bended ears-
In preparation for the unsuspected

Tip My Hat to the Tea Maker

A cup of tea if you please
What upon these waters flow?
A darkness
A discoloration so
Yet we tip to enjoy
Smooth flowing
A happier ending
Which seems to be repeated again and again
So it is in life my friend
We often go for the colored water-
Instead of the purified
One sustains for a moment
The other for life

Vapors

Adrift
Wind, a breeze, a mist
What is it that saturates our thought life?
What state of mind are we in?
It's the vapors
The atmosphere we set for ourselves
The thought processes
And from here we're guided in our decisions
What vapors?
What causes us to think what we think
And believe what we believe
And is what we believe worth believing?
Vapors set the tone for what's to come
But we get to decide-
The things hoped for and received

Success is a vapor; failure is a vapor
Having without complaining is a vapor
Favorable expectation, optimism, and hope are vapors
So are fear, poverty and defeat
We don't have to accept anything
Rather, we are able to set the tone for our lot in life
~ ~ ~ ~ ~ ~ ~

We have what we entertain!

People Pressure Me

Am I lost without reason, without hope?
Is there one I can turn to-
Other than the one many ascribe to
The _ _ _ _
With pressure comes a price-
If not handled correctly
If we are pressured let it be for seeking the truth
Knowing the truth
And not because of the pressures of life
For they only inflate to deflate...
Your person

Many Mouse

Many is the charge
Yet we cower in the corner as if it's our refuge
Or place of purpose
Many are called but few are chosen
Many are the blessings but few take notice
Many are the ways of sin
Which we give into time and time again
Lose some to gain some
So many can be found in me
For you
Blessings

Tailgate Party

Party if you will but lose your soul
Party the cares away-
Only to wake to their presence
Partying doesn't cure the ills
Or bring the greatest joy
In fact no joy
Only happiness for a time
And in time vague remembrance
I have a host of banquets for you to attend
Will you come?
Will you enjoy?
Or will you remain propped up on a house of cards-
With happiness as its host?

Passionate Life

Shall We Weep or Shall We Cry

Cry the tears
And do the tears benefit the cost
Let the tears flow for they grow once left
For in leaving they leave a deposit
A deposit which brings increase
Shall we weep or shall we cry
Cry a song
Weep a cry
Can we weep without crying
And cry the tears away?
Hear, hear
Hear slowly what I say
The tears bring joy once left
The departure of tears lifts and makes room-
For joy to enter in
The weeping and passionate draining
Yet maintaining the will when all seems lost
Weeping is crying
Yet not always in tears
Crying as though weeping
And yes the tears fall
Fall, fall, falling
Yet increasing all the more

Strong vs Weak

(Always playing the part, but never truly of the heart)

One is weak when he is unmoved with emotions
Never a sign of weakness
For it shows weakness
Unknown to him
Emotions display the greatest strength of all
A demanding way
His way or no way
For he is blinded by the sight of "self"
In it, through it, by it
There is no room for anyone else
Unless
Unless, they fit into his scheme of things
What does he bring-
Except confusion-
With conditions of nerves unsettled
In advertisement for the strong
He flaunts his physical strength
Pride is his prominent character
Yet inside
He is as defeated as a fighter who has never trained
Drained by hidden insecurities
Here's the man! Here's the man!
He's the man. He's the man.
So he thinks within his own mind
And never mindful of the things that truly matter
"All for nothing if not all for His will"

Upset Alley

Upset that the corners of life corner me
Am I allowed to leave if followed and trapped?
Am I happy about my circumstances or trapped?
Do I give up, give in, throw in the towel or fight?
Corners don't corner me, if you allow me

~ ~ ~ ~ ~ ~

Trapped by life?
The answer is in the call
Cry out and hear me answer
Fight, as truth will be your sweet surrender
For in crying out to me-
Ways of deliverance are made possible
Surely you have not been enslaved
400 yrs or even 70
If I delivered then, I do so now
The cry was great then
Let it be so now...
And your deliverance will be at hand

Frenetic Love

Up and down, crazy love
Sometimes sideway love
But still love
Unsettled; indescribable
Yet love
No matter how it comes
As long as its always recognized
As love

Most speed away the day
Never fully capturing the art of love
A slow and easy approach is best
In this, the smallest of moments are captured...
Yielding lasting fruit

Love the best way "we" know how
Until we come to realize & can exemplify His love
The greater love
The perfect love

Secretary Love

Love who you are in me
Live to be whom I created you to be
Then be
All that I am in you
Be
For it's not in asking or saying but doing
Be
All is well if you live in me and...
Be
Who I've called you to be

Watered-down Controversy

There will be controversy-
Which seems of little effect
But an even greater controversy
Is that our mind seems to remain closed-
To the truth

Pickled Fences

One to cross not to return
One who crossed, yet due to return
Return to Him and He will draw near
The fences
The dividing line between here and there
Somewhere vs. nowhere
And where else would you rather be-
Eternal glory satisfied-
Or forever forsaken by foolish pride?
The dividing line is the fence of love
Not so difficult to cross if the heart is willing

How Prideful are You

It's all about me
Have you not known?
Have you not seen?
That "I Am" the one who makes the seen, seen
It's all about me
So thoughts without thinking, in thinking
It's all about me

Pressure Counts

Count the time I have delivered
And know I will deliver still
Count the time-
When you could have departed prematurely-
To know the value of time
Even pressure has its purpose
For it counts
It counts in bringing out the best
Whereas...it
Whatever "it" is "in you"
Would never had risen

Still Open

Opportunities still open
A chance to try again, still open
Behind closed doors, steel bars
Still open
Opportunities exist
Even in the midst of everything that seems closed

Pumpkin Patch

The hidden truth often seems hidden
But it's here for all to see
In seeing one believes
And in believing-
One is set free

Wood Stock

The stocking of wood, no good
How so, if used for a source of fuel?
It burns and burns without lasting
Store up on the lasting
And the temporal will lose its flavor

Another Day in Paradise

Luxury liner, no cruise
All have gone adrift
A flavor for the finer things
Yet the finest of all exist
But often missed
Missed for a time in stolen time-
For the facade of a paradise is this

Count Down

Count down the time
And time will take away time-
Every time you try to add time
For it does not increase
How about now and then?
In the use of time-
Now is what matters most

Passionate Life

- Can you see the ocean, then see the sea?
  Much to live for
  Much to give
  More than a great name
  Is the message learned of love
  And to graciously show it abroad

- The difference between now and then is when

- Life is more important than work
  Unless our work is the type of life we live for

- Sometimes we're so busy counting coins
  We fail to notice the raining of bills

- A blemish on the record is one blotted out for life

- We can live without living, but are we willing to die
  to who we are?

- You can't be a tightwad tied to God

- With luck, nothing is won but hope

- A satisfied rope is a dangling prospect at best

- If we learn to bleed more we would plead more

- We take dives to dig deeper, not to lose

- A proper place is peace settled, resting

- Color me pretty if I succeed
  Color me blind if I don't follow
  Color me deaf if I shut my ears
  Color me unwise (foolish) if I mute the sound of
  salvation

Prosperous Pigeon

One flew, the other came
One meant to refrain, left
Another comes to glory
In the midst a gift is sent
Nonstop in its giving
Eternal in its living
More price is not necessary
For its paid in full
Now prosper if you will
For all of life is yours

Prosperous, Mighty

The mighty fall yet rise again
There is no depth to sin
Yet sin is not your home
Therefore roam
Roam with purpose
That you may cast a shadow of light
Night from light is that right?
Surely not!
As Light goes forth-
Left behind are the dark days of the past
Never to rise again
That's if you are risen with Him
The Christ

Paddle Me

Doors of discomfort spell doom
I have made room
Not to be broken
Except the heart and a contrite spirit-
Which are lifted up in me
My greatness is your gift
In that I bring comfort, hope and promise
Gravitate toward me-
And the broken things will mend
The heart healed, the body whole, the future bright
Seek me and see there are no limits
Only what you limit yourself in believing me for

Sugar Cane

Sugarcane medley
Sweet retreat
Not the eats
As if food can satisfy the buds
Much more to search for and seek after-
Should be the desire to love
For it leaves a taste, lasting

Seed Little

Seed a little
Seed a lot
What is
What is not
You make it to be what it shall be
Much or little
Little or much
The planting of seed brings forth a harvest
But how much?
You decide
For the rain falls where the dew has set
Little
Little
Yet much to be had
Pour some
Then some
More to be had
Not slack at all concerning his promises
Yet many are the passions that warm the heart
If it be a heart of compassion

Penguin Laughter

To laugh is to love again
To express is to show passion
To love is but our greatest gift

Possession of the Soul

Possessed, yes
By love
From above
Is there another?
I think not
This amidst the trials of life
In spite of the trials of life
Own him and you own life by Him
Love

Surviving

on

Make-Believe

Or

Awakened

to Truth

Surviving on Impulse

Impulse that takes your breath away
What a day, what a day!
Too many measure their days through emotions
Have I not settled the notion?
It's on the spirit one must rely
Instead of floundering in a sea of emotion
When one does-
The result is often sea sickness-
And unstable legs along the journey

A Place to Tell

Tell it all and you will be free
Tell me your lies and insecurities
Walls will be broken if the truth comes out
Deceiving only results in deceiving oneself
What is left?
Truth subdued and a foregone change within
Live a lie to tell the truth
Or live in truth to avoid lying
Repentance and righteousness go hand in hand
Tell the truth
And the covering of righteousness will keep you

A Step

A step for a time
Unchanged through time
A step to stop and go again
One shall refrain if the will is ready
One will leave never to return if his heart is unwilling
Will you leave me
Or leave all for me
My desire is for great things
Great peace, hope, outcome
Let the cry be great-
So the step taken will be toward me
In this, a change is brought forth
To change the time for all times
For it's a step made in freedom from sin

Small Bananas

Small fruit so sweet
Yet sweetness does not satisfy the buds
Only a taste to savor does
Allow your savor to be in favor of me-
Not a temporary tasting to the palate
Rather a needed change in taste for life

Closed View of Society

Closed-in view
Because we look not from the outside in
Instead, inside out
Change does start within
But so often we ought to take a step back-
To be able to see the greater picture unfolding
Oftentimes we chase the little mites-
And overlook the diabolical plans of deception
In this, we are mouse hunting
Instead of looking to prevent a plague
By not focusing on the greater issue at hand-
We are merely duck hunting
Rather than preparing-
For the great storm approaching

Craters

Fallen if falling not to return
Sometimes they do
But difficult is the journey
Better to have never fallen in the first place
Deliverance needed?
Deliverance is at hand-
In order to bypass the craters of the day
To experience life lived in its fullest
Rather than in time stolen
Combating the nature of sin

Decision Makes

Make the most of the moment
Each moment I have given you
Life is short
Breath even shorter
You may think as long as you have breath-
You have life
Not so
For everyone who is breathing is not living
Yet they are alive
But to what end?
Understand the end
Then you will value each breath taken

Gratifying Flesh

Can it be all that it seems?
The flesh and its enticements
Does it fill the itch once scratched?
Or is there an ongoing desire for more?
If so, more change is needed
Not like before
Consider change from the temporal to the eternal
From flesh to spirit
But the end of each makes its distinction
One leading to regret
And the other to reward
Both now and eternal

Deliverance Table

A basket for a time
This way, mine
His to lose, yours to gain
In losing His son He gained the world again
Furthermore His Son lives again
To reign again with Him is the offer given
Life is in Him
He gave all for all who would choose Him

Discomfort Corner

The good news
Deliverance is available
Peace, comfort available
Guidance, passion unfulfilled, delivered
It cost the price of salvation
Yes
Saying and confessing
Believing and receiving
And in receiving it comes
Desires in light of first desiring Him
Sometimes not so easy
But oh, so fair
All it takes is a receptive heart
For "The One" who gives-
Draws near to those who draw near
No fear in this
Unless, it's fear of Him reverently
For He alone holds the pattern
He alone is the source
By which one is delivered-
From the discomfort corner
A pattern of life
A pattern to live
This is the door to freedom to all that ails

Hollywood Shuffle

Shuffling of the mind in view
Once was, no longer is
The thought of you
Leaving passion for prison
That one might suffer instead of accepting freedom
Hollywood shuffle
A shuffle in matters of the heart
A form of truth destitute and destructive
A transformed life which is no life at all
In the end

Peaceable Laugh

Laugh
It's a fruit of happiness
Peace is kingdom rest amidst turmoil
Sometimes to get away...
We simply need to find ways that bring happiness
In doing so we're able to bear the burdens of life
A peaceable laugh-
Is to lay our burdens at the cross-
Not to pick them up again
In this the joys of life become available
Therefore laugh
Enjoy life
It's meant to be as such

Indecent Exposure

Exposure to blood, melting
A way of the world, felt
Desires unknown but kept
Kept until desires are made free, released
What's the choice?
Here's the choice
Believe
Believe more than just the seen-
Then you will see
Believe more than just a dream
Then it will be
Satisfy not the tongue at every turn
And the lesson to learn is this
Desires can be moving to indecent exposure
And the greater is to keep desires in control
By faith

Masters of Living

Some master living as if living is all
Some live to fall
Which is not living at all
There are some who are afraid of life
In this, they forfeit life
If without a cause why live?
There is purpose in this
In you
Find your purpose and you will find the value of life
Not what some make it to be
Rather, how it was meant to be
By me
In purpose
For life

Miserable City

The city of limits holds no boundaries-
From which I cannot deliver and set free
Free from lack and insufficiency
All is in me
Search for me with your whole heart-
And you will find me
And in finding me you find life
Free from everything binding and hindering
Trust me and see
What is there to lose-
Except an attempt to improve one's life

Potential Fun

The fun of life is to enjoy life and all its riches
There is a better level of living
Beyond feelings of gladness
Make me happy
Make me happy
The joys of life it brings
Who soothes the soul and stimulates the mind?
Surely not the happiest of days
Enjoy still
But let it not be for fun
For in time it fades away

Sacrifice Low

Low sacrifice
A sacrifice still
Some more than others
And some never will
Will you be my all?
If so
Answer the call
Of freedom with its many prizes
With the key prize being heaven
Sacrifice to show strength
Sacrifice to empower and to be empowered
Sacrifices yield the fruit of prosperity
Here and now
Then and thereafter
Master the art of sacrifice-
And I will show you a king at heart

Satisfy Spoil

Spoiled for a bit but alright
Ready to learn
Abandon the hide for the pride that tests the soul
No more his way, this way, that
All has come to order
And for the king-
He gave
He sat
No longer spoiled by the dictates past
Now is when
No longer then
For salvation has satisfied the soul

Sometimes We Test Patience

If patience was a test would we fail?
In waiting, do we wait unconsciously-
Or with expectation, anticipation and motion
One does not move until moved
Too often there is no movement
By this, one becomes stagnant
Furthermore a stench begins
Unless its of Him... to wait
But waiting involves more than nothing
Rather something to give while doing so
Therefore wait without being idle
For idleness stills the breeze of comfort -
Reared for the annals of life
Timing is everything
Sometimes nothing is better
But something always moves something-
Unless the intent is questionable
Therefore let nothing pass in waiting
For this type does not mean nothing
Rather waiting while progressively working...
Toward change

Beast Master

We master the beast
Rather the beast masters many
And many become the tool of his enjoyment
Look to the Son
Look to the Son
For the beast will eventually be slain

No Propaganda
Press Release

Let the truth ring out
Let the truth ring out
For every lie will have a defeat of its own

Son-less Life

No Son, no life
Life less ventured is life less attained
Moreover, refrained from life's fullest blessing
In essence, the fullness of life

The Nature of the Endgame

The nature of the endgame-
Is to impede, steal, thwart and destroy-
The prosperity I have stored
Not that it can be destroyed
But rather missed or forfeited
Because of negligence
Neglecting to focus on my word
Above the cares of life
The purpose of the endgame is to destroy hope
In hope of suppressing one's ability-
To realize and reach their full potential
The purpose of the endgame-
Is to muffle the voice of purpose-
So the call would not be received
The endgame is the devil's intent-
To keep men from finding out who they are
And who they can be
In God through Christ
The endgame is the game the enemy plays...
With destruction as its goal

The endgame
It's time we stop playing

Orleans Way

Orleans
A picture of New Orleans
A place where this world is coming to
Nothing withholding
No fantasy too far fetched
Where every desire can be fulfilled
All for a price
And the price many will pay-
Is not the debt they received
But an even greater is involved...
One's life
The price of fame, not worth it
For many have sold their soul and for what?
Only to die in the end
And all that was gain is lost
Even worse
Leading one to his or her death
The world is headed toward destruction
And it's the work of the remnant-
Who will make all the difference
A work for me, for the kingdom of God will suffice
Nothing less than the sacrifice of will-
So my will can be accomplished
Days are coming-
When the saved will have to show their true colors
Instead of teetering on the fence of indecision
Between the kingdom of God and this world
Let it all be for me
Let it all be for me

Needles

Needles, the pricks, the pins
What needles?
Those needles
Sometimes the poke from friends
Those who are closest aren't always so close
Not without a cause
Furthermore, some seek your attention-
In order to have their purposes lived out
Be careful whom you befriend
Sometimes the foe is prickly-
Though starting out as trustworthy

Doorway

From the front to the back
An opening and closing
One way, this way, that
To come or go
Enter or leave
What good is it and what matters?
One will need to enter the kingdom of God-
If they care to leave this world in a promising way
And even today live that way
The way out is the way in
So many leave before entering in
Open, wide open, always open
Is the door sign to the kingdom
Enter in that you might leave appropriately

The Ease of Life

The ease of life
Not so easy with strife...
Contention and misbehaving
The ease of life is a better life for those who learn
For those who leave...
This side for that
Yet staying to make a difference
There could be no better calling
No better purpose
Challenges and difficulties do come
Shall you not succeed, endure?
The price of life is death to self
Paid, is the price given
Now the "rest"
The "ease" meant to live in
Otherwise perdition

The light of God's glory -

Will shine brightly

In the lives of those who chose Him

The ease of life

Is a better life than the one before

No longer desperation

Fulfillment of promises and peace

Blessings released

A doomed end done away with

For the glory of His presence

The ease of life

A better life than before

And now what awaits-

Except the fate of a rewarding end

Beginning Now!

Raymond has truly put together a complimentary work in regards to the ultimate outlet for mundane living. He seeks to crack the banks of poverty in hope that a heavenly overflow of blessings might saturate both the inner man and all that encompasses his borders of being.

He is a chosen vessel who has been granted the privilege of presenting a divine doorway for better living, for Christians and nonbelievers alike.

There is no secret without safeguarding, but the secrets revealed here are for those who catch hold of the words within. Furthermore, the pathway remains uninformed, uninspired for those who disregard its message.

Raymond seeks to help others appropriate God's desire for each of us, which is to live the most meaningful and rewarding life possible while bringing him glory.

Inspired by truth and destined for the fullness of God's glory are the author, his words and the message given for those who are willing to receive.